ETERNAL SECURITY AND THE BIBLE

As Seen by a Layman

by
Samuel R. Harding

SCHMUL PUBLISHING COMPANY
NICHOLASVILLE, KENTUCKY

Published by Schmul Publishing Co.
PO Box 776
Nicholasville, KY 40340

Printed in the United States of America

ISBN 10: 0-88019-059-0
ISBN 13: 978-0-88019-059-6

Visit us on the Internet at www.wesleyanbooks.com, or order direct from the publisher by calling 800-772-6657, or by writing to the above address.

This book is dedicated to my faithful wife

whose valuable contribution is hidden in every page. During the past three summer vacations, as we enjoyed God's great outdoors together by camping in a number of beautiful parks, we continued our work on this project.

Even with a fly or mosquito putting in a "plug" now and then it was nice to have this to work on when we got tired of resting.

INTRODUCTION

Here is a study of one hundred thirty-five Scriptures in twenty-six books of the Bible. Because of the superficial thinking and rationalizing going on today, this book is very timely and ought to have a wide circulation. I bespeak for it a very helpful ministry. The author has been faithful to the general tenor of the Scriptures. He has not chosen a few isolated verses to prove a pet doctrine of his own.

The author, Samuel R. Harding, is a member of the faculty of the College of Engineering at the State University of Iowa. For many years he served as the faculty advisor for the student Inter-Varsity Christian Fellowship on the university campus. He is an active Christian layman in his own denomination on both the local and the national levels. He is currently serving his local church as a member of its Board of Publications.

One of the greatest needs of the Christian world today is a more careful and sincere study of the Bible. The author has thus used a great deal of God's Word in presenting the position which he holds relative to the matter of unconditional eternal security. He shows clearly how the Christian is secure in Christ but very insecure apart from Christ in wilful continuous sinning. Read this book to be informed and practice its teachings to be secure.

Dr. Myron F. Boyd, A.B., LI.B., D.D.

Director and Speaker of the
Light and Life Radio Hour
Winona Lake, Indiana

PREFACE

During my early life I had no close contact with fellow Christians who hold the doctrine now commonly known as "eternal security." Except as I occasionally saw it mentioned in print, it was seldom brought to my attention. Then, suddenly, upon moving to a different community, I became aware that eternal security was accepted by more fundamental Christian people than I had realized. I also found that I was not well informed as to all that is included in the doctrine; neither did I know what Biblical ground was claimed for either its approval or rejection.

I became very much interested in learning exactly what the Bible does say on this subject. We all know that the important thing is what God says about a doctrine, not what you or I may think about it.

For several years my wife and I have studied the Bible together in a prayerful, earnest effort to determine what God actually does say about the eternal destiny of a person who was once saved, but who later goes into a life of sin and never again comes back to God in sincere repentance.

This book is based upon these years of Bible study.

Being a layman I am at both a disadvantage and at an advantage. I am at a disadvantage because I have not had theological and seminary training. I am at an advantage because my personal thinking on this subject has not been colored, or influenced, by classroom teachers of either of the opposing schools of thought.

In harmony with the statement that the important thing is to know what God says, you will find Part II of this book made up largely of Bible quotations of which, as you know, **God is the author.**

ACKNOWLEDGMENT

A number of people, including several well known ministers, have been kind enough to give the manuscript for this book a very thoughtful reading. Their suggestions have been much appreciated and were often incorporated into the work. A number of others have also given the author valuable assistance. To all these people the author expresses his sincere appreciation.

Samuel R. Harding
Iowa City, Iowa

TABLE OF CONTENTS

PART I

The Author's Views on Questions Relating to
The Doctrine of Eternal Security

PART II

**Bible Passages and Scriptural Teachings Relating to
The Doctrine of Eternal Security**

PART III

Basic Deductions From Our Study of
The Doctrine of Eternal Security

ADDENDA

List of Bible passages to which reference is made in
    this book.
    (In most instances the passages are quoted in
full.)

INFORMATION RELATING TO
THE DOCTRINE OF ETERNAL SECURITY

What is the historical background of the eternal security doctrine?

John Calvin (1509-1564), a French Protestant reformer, is often considered the father of this doctrine of eternal security, although there is evidence that a very similar teaching existed in Bible times.

Was the eternal security doctrine the only doctrine Calvin emphasized?

No. Another doctrine Calvin taught ardently is the doctrine of "election," that only those elected by God to be saved could be saved. All others **must** be lost.

It is not as commonly known that Calvin also taught "infant damnation"—most people dying in infancy were lost.

Does the person who today identifies himself as a "Calvinist" mean that he believes in eternal security, election, and infant damnation?

No, most likely not. Most of them would hold up their hands in horror at infant damnation and comparatively few still hold to election. These doctrines of

Calvin, though taught by his followers for some years, failed to have the popular appeal enjoyed by the eternal security doctrine.

What then is meant when it is said that a certain person is a "Calvinist"?

It often means no more than that he believes in Calvin's doctrine of eternal security.

What is meant when it is said that a certain person is an "Arminian"?

Jacobus Arminius (1560-1609), a Dutch Protestant theologian, strongly opposed certain doctrines of Calvinism, especially "final perseverance of the saints," commonly known today as eternal security. Therefore one who rejects Calvin's doctrine of eternal security is frequently referred to as an Arminian.

PART I

THE AUTHOR'S VIEWS
ON QUESTIONS RELATING TO
THE DOCTRINE OF ETERNAL SECURITY

PART I

What is the doctrine of eternal security?

Three common forms of the doctrine of eternal security are given below.

a. That one who is really "born again," and therefore a child of God, will not be lost eternally regardless of how deeply he may go into sin and die in his sins.

b. That people who are really saved will eventually come back to God before they die, even though they may wander into sin for a time.

c. That living a life of sin, after a profession of conversion, is evidence that the individual never was saved.

With which form of eternal security teaching are we mainly concerned?

Except when otherwise stated, with the first form, form a.

What does eternal security teach regarding the punishment of the backslider who dies in his sins?

Eternal security teaches that the unrepentant backslider will suffer only loss of reward. It teaches he will enter heaven as a **saint**, but short of some rewards.

What does eternal security teach about the "free moral agency of man"?

Eternal security recognizes that man is saved only as he exercises his privilege as a free moral agent, and makes his decision to repent and seek salvation. It teaches that after man is once a saved man he cannot choose to leave God. It teaches that he is no longer a free moral agent so far as salvation is concerned. A man once saved could not avoid heaven if he wanted to and will go to heaven no matter how wicked a life he lives.

What does eternal security teach regarding the backslider who becomes an extremely vile sinner?

Eternal security often teaches that in some cases a backslider becomes so wicked that God takes him to his home in heaven prematurely. He becomes such a liability on earth that to protect God's kingdom on earth God takes this vile man to heaven before his time. (I remember how shocked I was when I learned this was included in the teaching. I have heard, and read, it a number of times.)

What is claimed for the doctrine of eternal security?

Those who believe this doctrine of eternal security state that it gives them wonderful peace of mind.

They are at ease because they say the entire responsibility for their salvation, after conversion, rests alone upon God. They hold that nothing they do in the future will affect their eternal destiny. They say that since salvation is of God and not of man, man would be saving himself if he had any part in his salvation.

Eternal security people often say that were it not for this doctrine they would be most disturbed if not distracted, for fear they might fall and be lost.

Why be concerned about what others believe regarding the doctrine of eternal security?

There is an abundant evidence that many a person, **now living a life of sin**, is convinced he **is** a saved man. He honestly believes he was once saved and thus became a possessor of "eternal life." He has been taught that eternal life being "eternal" is an irrevocable ticket to heaven. He believes he **can not be lost** regardless of how he lives.

One may say that he who goes back into a life of sin, after he thought he was saved, was never really saved. It may be that he was never saved but he really believes he was. He has been taught that he is eternally secure and he is staking his eternal destiny on his faith in this doctrine. Such a man may be eternally lost because of this doctrine. It keeps him from seeking a proper relationship with God.

How careful should one be before accepting and teaching a doctrine?

It is not enough that some passages of Scripture

seem to support a doctrine. If the doctrine affects the eternal destiny of men one should not promote it until an extensive study of the Bible convinces him that there is **absolutely no possibility of this doctrine being in error.**

Who should receive the greater condemnation? Backslider or sinner?

To me it is unthinkable and unscriptural that one who has been a member of God's Kingdom and who has enjoyed the blessing of the Christian life, then deliberately turned traitor, should enter eternal glory, whereas his companion in sin who has never been a member of the Kingdom is lost.

What is my message to all backsliders?

I pray most earnestly that all backslider readers, **feeling** secure because they are convinced they were once saved, will see that, according to the Scripture, they are clinging to nothing but a **false hope of heaven.** One of my greatest reasons for writing is to reach such people with what God really says on this subject, and thus help to bring such backsliders back to Him. May the Holy Spirit be your companion as you search His Word for the truth.

What is my personal attitude toward people who believe the doctrine of eternal security?

May I assure you that this Bible study on the subject of eternal security is being written in a most friendly spirit. I have true Christian love for born-again believers whose views on this subject are contrary to my own.

Many, many eternal security people live most exemplary and godly lives, even though they believe such is not necessary for salvation.

I have no desire to argue with anyone. I want to present the Word of God as I am convinced the Holy Spirit would have me present it. I invite those who differ with me to prayerfully study God's Word with me. May this study of His Holy Word prove a blessing to all of us.

It is to be regretted deeply that many times writers on both sides of this subject stoop to belittling the individual who holds the opposite view. It is my desire that this writing be entirely free from any such unfriendly spirit. I love my sincere Christian brother who honestly differs with me on this subject, but I must reserve the right to differ with him in doctrine, because I believe it to be a dangerous doctrine contrary to the correct understanding of the Word of God.

Should we avoid discussing eternal security because it is so often considered a controversial subject?

We are often told that eternal security is a controversial subject and thus, for the sake of harmony in the church, we should avoid its discussion. What Bible truth is not a controversial subject? The virgin birth of Christ, the second coming of Christ, the atonement, and any doctrine one might mention are controversial subjects with certain people. Should I keep still when I find a friend, possibly a brother church member, teaching a doctrine I believe is responsible for souls being lost? I admit that in the past I have, for the sake of harmony, sometimes remained silent on this subject. I am becoming convicted for doing so. Why should I hesitate to teach what, after a careful study of the Bible, I am convinced is true Bible doctrine? Let's put it this way: How do I dare remain silent when I believe the salvation of souls is an issue? May the Holy Spirit direct me to say what I should, when I should, and say it in a true Christ-like spirit.

Would "eternal life" be "eternal" if one might possess it for a time only?

It is often said that "eternal life is eternal and therefore can never be lost." It is also said that if it could be lost it would not be eternal.

In I John 5:11, 12 we find these words, "And this is the record, that God hath given to us eternal life, and this life is in his Son. He that hath the Son hath life; and **he that hath not the Son of God hath not life.**" (Surely eternal life is the only kind of life being referred to in this passage.) This quotation from the Bible tells us that **eternal life is in God's Son** and the way we become possessors of eternal life is by Christ indwelling in our lives. Therefore if Christ goes out of our lives eternal life goes out, too. Eternal life IS eternal, but we cease to be the possessors of it if we let Christ go out of our lives. Who would dare suggest that Christ is indwelling in a drunken backslider or in anyone living a life of sin?

Can one depend upon "catchy" phrases and slogans?

No doubt political campaigns and other important

issues are often won by the side which can invent the most catchy slogans. People have a habit of accepting such slogans without thinking them through.

How often we hear "Once a son always a son" or "After one has been born he cannot be unborn." I am convinced that, with some people, slogans like these carry far more weight than all the Bible passages on the subject combined. Why do I think so? Because they are quoted frequently in preference to quotations from the Bible.

Let us analyze this first slogan, "Once a son always a son." In the first place we must be careful when we attempt to support a doctrine with a physical illustration. The spiritual realm and the physical realm are far from identical. Take, for example, the fact that one's physical birth takes place without the individual's knowledge or approval. He has absolutely no voluntary part in it himself. Would anyone even suggest that such is true concerning the spiritual birth, the "new birth"? Since we become sons of God only upon the proper exercise of our own will we DO have a part to play in our salvation. Why is it considered so very unreasonable that we remain sons of God by the same exercise of our will, as free moral agents?

If the slogan "Once a son always a son" expressed Biblical truth regarding the new birth, there could be no salvation for any of us, because, were we not children of Satan before we became children of God? In speaking to certain unsaved men of His day on earth, Christ said, "Ye are of your father the devil" (John 8:44a). If this slogan is correct there could be no salvation for these men for whom Christ came to die. (Please see Part II for further study of John 8:44).

Also in the third chapter of Luke there are sixteen

verses which are used to give the earthly genealogy of Jesus. Verse twenty-three starts with Jesus and verse thirty-eight includes Adam, but there is something most interesting and unexpected here. The genealogy does not stop with Adam, the first man. It says Adam "was the son of God." If the statement "Once a son always a son" were true, Adam never lost that sonship. If Adam never lost that sonship he did not need a "Redeemer." The death of Christ was therefore unnecessary. Do you realize that when you use the apparently harmless little phrase, "Once a son always a son," you are unintentionally telling God He did not need to send His Son to redeem man?

Is sinning to be condoned?

It is often said that Christians sin every day and that we cannot live without sinning. This is not a treatise on sin, but surely we all recognize that there is a vast difference between the one who, upon the realization of sin in his life, earnestly repents of it and who is determined by God's grace to live a pure life, and the one who deliberately lives in sin day after day, never repenting of it.

Even before the dispensation of grace it was possible for people to live "blameless" before the Lord. Speaking of Zacharias and Elisabeth, Luke tells us, "They were both righteous before God, walking in all the commandments and ordinances of the Lord blameless" (Luke 1:6). This does not say they were blameless in the sight of their neighbors, but do you suppose anyone would have thought of applying the term "sinning saints" to them?

Is your "feeling" of security founded upon the "fact" of security?

Since man's fall he has been seeking security. Adam attempted to find it by trying to hide from God. The building of the tower of Babel was inspired by such a desire. Witness also the fortified castles and city walls of old, and the modern military equipment of today.

It is often forgotten that there may be a "feeling" of security when the "fact" of security does not exist. Some years ago, when working on a house, I had occasion to work on a scaffold with which I was unfamiliar. I checked it carefully. As I first walked back and forth on the planks, and shook the scaffold, I held onto the building. Only after I was fully convinced I was "secure" did I go to work, and that with complete confidence. I soon learned that my "feeling" of security was not enough. The scaffold crumbled and the doctor took stitches in my head. This is but one example of thousands of people who had a "feeling" of security when the "fact" of security did not exist. Many have been injured physically or have lost their lives because their "feeling" of security was not based upon the "fact" of security.

If you are enjoying a feeling of eternal security be sure your feeling is based upon the fact of Bible security. I personally am enjoying a wonderful feeling of eternal security. I don't question my salvation, or live in fear I may be lost. I enjoy the wonderful "witness of the Spirit" that my sins are forgiven and that my name is recorded in the "Lamb's Book of Life." However, the Bible teaches that it would be possible for me to go into a life of sin and be lost eternally.

When I make this last statement to some people

they exclaim, "Oh! If I believed that way I would have no rest or peace of mind." Wait a minute. Let us apply to our spiritual lives what everyone knows regarding his physical life.

Between my home and my place of employment is a river. One morning as I was going to work, I joined a crowd of people at the railing of the bridge. Directly below was a patch of water surrounded by rather thin ice. Beneath the surface of the water was the body of a young man who had deliberately, and of his own free choice, climbed over the protecting railing and plunged into the river.

The bridge afforded adequate "security." Thousands of people cross it daily. This individual made a wrong use of the free power of choice that God had given him.

Do you suppose that ever since this happened, I stop before crossing that bridge and hesitate to cross it for fear I too will climb over the rail and take my own life? I have the same power of choice that the young man had. Would anyone insist that before he crosses that bridge, or any other bridge, that the railing must be built so high that he cannot possibly climb over it? When I retire at night do I stay awake for fear that the next morning I may ignore the protection the bridge affords or that I may take my own life through some other way?

Why will some people insist that to have peace of mind they must be so protected that they cannot commit spiritual suicide although they recognize that they may take their own physical life any time they may want to but never worry a whit about ever wanting to do so?

There is such a thing as the "fact" of security. God's Word assures us of abundant security provided we take advantage of such security. We must accept His plan of salvation which includes departing from iniquity, and living righteous lives. "If I regard iniquity in my heart, the Lord will not hear me" (Psalm 66:18). God compels no one to be saved against his will. To save the man who has wilfully departed from God in this life is forcing salvation upon him just as much as though God saved all men without their ever repenting.

If you are depending upon a feeling of security be SURE that your feeling is based upon the fact of Bible security.

What types in the Old Testament shed light on the subject of eternal security?

Both Calvinists and Arminians make much of "being covered by the blood." It is well that they do for this is the foundation of our Christian faith.

We all recognize that the passover lamb is a definite type of Christ. The Israelite was to choose the passover lamb (Exodus 12:3-5). He was to apply the blood (Exodus 12:7). Then note, **he had to remain under its protection** until the judgment of God had been executed (Exodus 12:22). "None of you shall go out at the door of his house until the morning." He was protected only as he **voluntarily remained** under the protection of the blood.

Another Old Testament type is the city of refuge (Numbers 35). It was not enough for the man to flee to the city of refuge. He had to **remain there until the death of the high priest.** Christ is our High Priest. Our High Priest does not die. The deduction is evident.

What is the difference between "assurance" and "eternal security"?

Some people are surprised that one can have complete peace of mind and soul even though he does not accept the doctrine of eternal security. I have referred to the fact that I enjoy full "assurance" of sins forgiven and that I am SURE I am a child of God. I am trusting in the cleansing and keeping power of the blood of Christ **in which I have full confidence.** I do have a part in my salvation and my part is to take advantage of the unlimited power God provides for me, but does not force upon me against my will. Christ is the Way (the bridge, if you please) but I **must stay in the Way,** (not leap over the protecting railing) if I am to make heaven my home.

We have **assurance** of salvation when, as a result of obeying God, we repent of sin and live according to His plan for us. No, friend, we are not "saved today and lost tomorrow, never knowing where we stand" as some insist. We enjoy wonderful peace with God, "assurance" built upon a sound foundation.

A feeling of security may be based upon a false premise: "Assurance" is the witness of the Holy Spirit that one is right with God. The Holy Spirit makes no mistakes (Romans 8:16).

Why do people believe as they do?

"They were taught that way" is usually the answer as to why people believe as they do. How few people do any real **searching** of the Bible for themselves.

Have YOU, regardless of how you believe on this

eternal security question, ever taken your Bible and with as unbiased mind as possible studied **prayerfully** this subject of eternal security? Have you tried to forget that you would like to believe as you do? Are you willing to admit that you may be wrong?

The failure of many good Christian people to study the Bible for themselves **has resulted in thousands of them being convinced that all sorts of false cults are right** and has enabled these cults to flourish. Remember, most of them claim to base their teaching on the Bible. If you listen to one line of teaching only, you are very likely to eventually come to believe that way, regardless of how false that teaching may be. Again I say, **search the Bible for yourself.**

Another reason why people believe as they do is that "They want to believe that way." Without doubt the eternal security teaching appeals to many who are not willing to give up certain sins, but who still want to believe they are saved. It is nice too to feel that a backslidden relative or friend, living in sin, is still saved.

Why do people often give more weight to man's statement of what a Bible passage means than to the plain untampered passage itself?

The answer to this question is related closely to what has just been said about why people believe as they do. In many cases a man will find in the Bible what **he wants to find in it.**

What question should every one of us ask himself?

Regarding each doctrine he believes one should ask himself, "Do I believe this doctrine because I have made a careful, independent study of the doctrine or because I have heard this doctrine taught more than doctrines which are in opposition to it?"

Should an eternal security believer hesitate to examine the Bible extensively relative to his doctrine?

If the doctrine of eternal security is true, it can not suffer by comparing it with the passages of Scripture found in Part II of this book, or with any other portions of Scripture. If it should fail to stand up against such an examination it would be tragic to hold it.

In all spheres of life, the important thing is not to **prove that we are right,** but to determine IF we are right. He who does not dare to examine evidence is fearful that it may prove him to be wrong. This would result in humiliation of pride. The natural urge is to shut one's eyes to what does not please him. Truth is not arrived at this way.

The attitude of too many people is expressed by the man who said, "Don't bother me with the facts, my mind is already made up."

How can one test a doctrine to see if it is true or false?

Here are four basic tests which should be put to every doctrine.

1. Does this doctrine flow from the Bible naturally? Is it in harmony with the most direct understanding of **the entire Bible?**

2. Does the support of this doctrine require strained and awkward interpretations of Scripture?

3. Is this doctrine in complete harmony with God's evaluation and abhorrence of sin, and His plan of redemption?

4. Does this doctrine encourage a closer walk with God rather than to encourage yielding to temptation and a life of sin?

As you study the Bible portions which are quoted in Part II of this book, please check the eternal security doctrine with these four tests and determine for yourself where it stands.

PART II

BIBLE PASSAGES AND SCRIPTURAL

TEACHINGS RELATING TO THE

DOCTRINE OF ETERNAL SECURITY

PART II

Does the Bible teach that those who have eternal life shall never perish, and that no one can pluck them out of God's hand?

> "My sheep hear my voice, and I know
> them, and they follow me: And I give unto
> them eternal life; and they shall never
> perish, neither shall any man pluck them
> out of my hand" (John 10:27, 28).

I know of no passage which is used more frequently than this to teach saved people they can never be lost. The last part of the passage (verse 28 only) is most often used alone. It reads, "And I give unto them eternal life; and they shall never perish, neither shall any man pluck them out of my hand."

Please notice the grammatical construction of these two verses. Neither one, alone, is a complete sentence. Quoting one without the other is an attempt to get a correct meaning from a sentence by ignoring a related part of the same sentence. I am sure that most people who use the last part of this sentence alone do not realize how closely it is related to the first part of the sentence.

Verse 27, the first part of this sentence, states clearly to whom the wonderful promises in verse 28, the last part of this same sentence, apply. It is most evident the promises are for "My sheep," those Christ owns as His own. Christ looked down through the ages and saw that many to whom the promises do not apply would try to claim them for themselves. He therefore clearly defines His sheep. He definitely limits them to those that "hear my voice" and "follow me." If you are not listening to the voice of Christ and following Him, how can you possibly, by any stretch of the imagination, think that Christ considers you one of His sheep? Certainly no one can sincerely say that a backslider, living a life of sin, is following Christ. Christ does **not** lead us into sin.

How about the promises themselves, "shall never perish" and "neither shall any man pluck them out of my hand"? Like all Bible promises, these promises are conditional. While we are listening to the voice of Christ and following Him we will not perish and neither can any man reach in and pluck us out of Christ's protecting hand. What more could anyone need? The devil himself can't reach in and snatch us out. We are absolutely safe while in His hand. What is overlooked by many, though, is that there is nothing here which annuls our freedom to leave that wonderful place of protection. This we do if we **cease** to listen to Christ's voice and cease to follow Him. The experience of salvation does not rob man of his free moral agency.

Is it possible for a saved person to "fall from grace" or backslide?

"Christ is become of no effect unto you,
whosoever of you are justified by the law;
ye are fallen from grace" (Galatians 5:4).

Why do we have this passage if one cannot fall?

"I will therefore put you in remembrance, though ye once knew this, how that the Lord, **having saved the people out of the land of Egypt, afterward destroyed them that believed not**" (Jude 5).

If Jude is not teaching that saved people can fall and be eternally lost, what is he teaching?

"Thou wilt say then, The branches were broken off, that I might be graffed in. Well: **because of unbelief they were broken off,** and thou standest by faith. Be not highminded, but fear: For if God spared not the natural branches, take heed lest he also spare not thee. Behold therefore the goodness and severity of God: on them which fell, severity; but toward thee, goodness, if thou continue in his goodness; otherwise thou also shalt be cut off" (Romans 11:19-22).

We are living in a day when it is popular to mention the goodness of God but very unpopular to mention the "severity" of God. The severity of God is referred to in this warning to the Gentile Christians that since God spared not the Jews, His chosen people, the Gentiles certainly could not expect to be an exception, if they refused to obey God.

Is it possible for one's name to be blotted out of God's book of life?

"He that overcometh, the same shall be

clothed in white raiment; and I will **not blot out his name out of the book of life,** but I will confess his name before my Father, and before his angels" (Revelation 3:5).

Eternal security teaches that if one's name is once placed in the "book of life" it can never be blotted out. If that were true, this verse has no place in the Bible. Why say that "He that overcometh" will not have his name blotted out if all names are to remain in the book of life even though their owners do not "overcome"?

"And the Lord said unto Moses, **Whosoever hath sinned against me, him will I blot out of my book**" (Exodus 32:33).

The children of Israel had sinned in making and worshipping the golden calf, thus forsaking God. In earnestly praying for the people Moses had said to God, "Yet now, if thou wilt forgive their sin—; and if not, blot me, I pray thee, out of thy book which thou hast written" (Exodus 32:32).

I fail to reconcile Moses' prayer and God's answer, "Whosoever hath sinned against me, him will I blot out of my book," with the eternal security teaching that no names can be blotted out of God's book.

Is there any evidence that repentance, at the time of conversion, includes repentance for sins which may be committed after that time?

"Whom God hath set forth to be a propitiation through faith in his blood, to

declare his righteousness for the remission
of sins that are past, through the
forbearance of God; To declare, I say, at
this time his righteousness: that he might
be just, and the justifier of him which
believeth in Jesus" (Romans 3:25, 26).

We are told here that when we come to Jesus He
forgives the sins that are past. Repentance is an essen-
tial element, or condition to salvation. How can one
sincerely repent of a future sin?
Eternal security assumes that when one repents
of past sins he automatically repents of all sins he may
commit in the future. I find absolutely nothing in
God's Word to support this teaching.

**Must one continue to believe, or might one accept
Christ and later reject Him and still be saved?**

"Jesus said unto her, I am the resurrection,
and the life: he that believeth in me, though
he were dead, yet shall he live: And whosoever liveth and believeth in me shall never
die" (John 11:25, 26a).

Notice the present tense, "liveth" and
"believeth." Christ did not tell Martha that all who
had at one time believed on Him would never die. The
Williams translation reads, "Whosoever continues to
believe in me."

"Verily, verily, I say unto you, He that
believeth on me hath everlasting life" (John
6:47).
"Verily, verily, I say unto you, He that

heareth my word, and **believeth** on him that sent me, hath everlasting life, and shall not come into condemnation; but is passed from death unto life" (John 5:24).

Jesus emphasizes the thought in these two statements by saying "verily, verily." In both cases the present tense for believing is used.

Who really are children of God, or "sons of God"?

"For as many as are **led by the Spirit of God, they are the sons of God**" (Romans 8:14).

Is one who is "out of fellowship with God" being led by the Spirit of God? Certainly not. Then how can he still claim to be a "son of God"?

"**But if any man love God, the same is known of him**" (I Corinthians 8:3).

God recognizes as His own those who love Him. A life of sin does not express love for God.

"**He that overcometh** shall inherit all things; and I will be his God, and **he shall be my son**" (Revelation 21:7).

If you want God to consider you His son it is necessary for you to so live that He will consider you an "overcomer," not a backslider.

"But whoso **keepeth his word**, in him

verily is the love of God perfected: **hereby
know we that we are in him**" (I John 2:5).

Those who are living in sin are thus excluded from
the body of Christ.

"**And they that are Christ's have crucified
the flesh** with the affections and lusts"
(Galatians 5:24).

This is the Bible's standard for one who belongs
to Christ.

"But in every nation **he that feareth him,
and worketh righteousness, is accepted with
him**" (Acts 10:35).

To be accepted as one of God's children one must
"fear" God, and work righteousness. "Fear" as used
in this way implies reverence and obedience.

"And being made perfect, he became the
author of **eternal salvation unto all them
that obey him;** Called of God an high priest
after the order of Melchisedec" (Hebrews
5:9, 10).

What is "eternal salvation" if it is not eternal life?
To whom is Christ the author of eternal salvation, or
eternal life? This Scripture passage gives the answer,
"unto all them that obey him." How can one who is
not obeying Christ think he qualifies for eternal life?
Can such an one consider himself a child of God?

"My little children, these things write I

unto you, **that ye sin not.** And if any man sin, we have an advocate with the Father, Jesus Christ the righteous: And he is the propitiation for our sins: and not for ours only, but also for the sins of the whole world. But **whoso keepeth his word,** in him verily is the love of God perfected: **hereby know we that we are in him**" (I John 2:1, 2, 5).

Who belongs to God? "Whoso keepeth his word."

"If we say that we have fellowship with him, and walk in darkness, we lie, and do not the truth: But **IF we walk in the light,** as he is in the light, we have fellowship one with another, and **the blood of Jesus Christ his Son cleanseth us from all sin**" (I John 1:6, 7).

Under what conditions does the blood of Jesus Christ cleanse from sin? The answer is, "IF we walk in the light as he is in the light." It is evident that to qualify as one of God's children one must "walk in the light."

"And when he putteth forth his own sheep, he goeth before them, and **the sheep follow him:** for they know his voice" (John 10:4).

As in John 10:27, 28, Jesus is certainly teaching that just as a shepherd's own sheep followed the shepherd, Jesus' own sheep follow Him. Following Jesus is evidence we are His. Also, He is teaching just as strongly, by inference, that the sheep who do not follow the shepherd do not belong to that shepherd. Of course those who do not follow Jesus have no right to claim they are His.

Who definitely does NOT belong to God?

> "Now **if any man have not the Spirit of Christ, he is none of his**" (Romans 8:9c).

Does the so-called "sinning saint" have the Spirit of Christ?

> "**He that is not with me is against me;**" (Matthew 12:30a).

Is the backslider with Christ or against Him? Can one who is against God rightfully claim he belongs to God?

> Whosoever transgresseth, and **abideth not in the doctrine of Christ, hath not God.** He that abideth in the doctrine of Christ, he hath both the Father and the Son" (II John 9).

What could be plainer than the words in bold type in the passage above?

> "He that **committeth sin is of the devil;** for the devil sinneth from the beginning. For this purpose the Son of God was manifested, that he might destroy the works of the devil. **Whosoever is born of God doth**

not commit sin; for his seed remaineth in him: and he cannot sin, because he is born of God. In this the children of God are manifest, and the children of the devil: **whosoever doeth not righteousness is not of God,** neither he that loveth not his brother" (I John 3:8-10).

Possibly the Holy Spirit has not yet revealed the entire meaning of this passage to anyone. Please remember though that ALL of it is the Word of God. Our understandings of just what constitutes sin may differ considerably. Certainly one is safe, though, when he says that the act of living in a backslidden state is sin. This passage states emphatically that "He that committeth sin is of the devil." Heaven is not to be filled with the devil's people.

> **"Ye are of your father the devil,** and the lusts of your father ye will do" (John 8:44a).

The Jews to whom Christ spoke these words had just told Him, "We have one Father, even God." Jesus corrected them with this contradictory statement, **"Ye are of your father the devil."** Jesus also told them, "If God were your Father, ye would love me" (verse 42a).

Two truths stand out in the quotations of Jesus;

1. Unless our lives show we love Christ we can not rightfully lay claim to being sons of God.

2. Since Christ was preaching salvation for these very people whom He considered sons of the devil, it is evidently possible, in the spiritual realm, to change spiritual fathers. How wonderful that we can, by the

grace of God, cease to be sons of the devil and become sons of God. (As stated in Part I of this book, if the phrase "once a son always a son" were true in the spiritual realm, there could be no salvation for anyone.)

Who definitely does NOT have eternal life?

"And Jesus said unto him, No man, **having put his hand to the plough, and looking back, is fit for the kingdom of God**" (Luke 9:62).

Is the bride of Christ to be made up of people who are not fit for the kingdom of God?

"For this ye know, that **no whoremonger, nor unclean person, nor covetous man,** who is an idolater, **hath any inheritance in the kingdom of Christ and of God**" (Ephesians 5:5).

When speaking of the resurrection Jesus said, "**and they that have done evil, unto the resurrection of damnation**" (John 5:29c).

"Now the works of the flesh are manifest, which are these; **Adultery, fornication, uncleanness, lasciviousness, idolatry, witchcraft, hatred, variance, emulations, wrath, strife, seditions, heresies, Envyings, murders, drunkenness, revellings,** and such like: of the which I tell you before, as I have also told you in time past, that **they which do such things shall not inherit the kingdom of God**" (Galatians 5:19-21).

"Know ye not that the **unrighteous shall
not inherit the kingdom of God? Be not**
deceived: neither fornicators, nor idolaters,
nor adulterers, nor effeminate, nor abusers
of themselves with mankind, nor thieves,
nor covetous, nor drunkards, nor revilers,
nor extortioners, shall inherit the kingdom
of God" (I Corinthians 6:9, 10).

We sometimes hear people say that they believe in
eternal security but not in an extreme view of it. They
say they take a middle ground. (I looked in vain
through all these passages for any indication of a possible middle ground, or any hint of an exception for the
backslider who is guilty of such sins as mentioned in
these passages.) Other people admit that the eternal
security doctrine teaches that all people mentioned in
the passages quoted above—fornicators, adulterers,
drunkards, et cetera—are children of God, if they have
once been saved. They admit that their teaching
demands that when Christ comes to call His own, such
people will be caught up from brothels, taverns, and all
dens of iniquity to become a part of the spotless bride
of Christ. I ask how can such a doctrine be true when
the Bible states clearly and definitely that such people
"shall not inherit the kingdom of God"?

**When we are saved, is our salvation so complete and
fixed that there is nothing more required of us?**

"For now we live, IF ye stand fast in
the Lord" (I Thessalonians 3:8). "For we are
made partakers of Christ, IF we hold the
beginning of our confidence stedfast unto

the end" (Hebrews 3:14). "Then said Jesus to those Jews which believed on him, IF ye continue in my word, then are ye my disciples indeed;" (John 8:31). "But Christ as a son over his own house; whose house are we IF we hold fast the confidence and the rejoicing of the hope firm unto the end" (Hebrews 3:6).

"Moreover, brethren, I declare unto you the gospel which I preached unto you, which also ye have received, and wherein ye stand; By which also ye are saved, IF ye keep in memory what I preached unto you, unless ye have believed in vain" (I Corinthians 15:1, 2).

"Let that therefore abide in you, which ye have heard from the beginning. IF that which ye have heard from the beginning shall remain in you, ye also shall continue in the Son, and in the Father. And this is the promise that he hath promised us, even eternal life" (I John 2:24, 25).

"And you, that were sometime alienated and enemies in your mind by wicked works, yet now hath he reconciled in the body of his flesh through death, to present you holy and unblameable and unreproveable in his sight. IF ye continue in the faith grounded and settled, and be not moved away from the hope of the gospel, which ye have heard, and which was preached to every creature which is under heaven; whereof I Paul am made a minister;" (Colossians 1:21-23).

Steadfastness, and "continuing in the faith," being "firm unto the end," "standing fast in the Lord," are all required after salvation.

> "And hereby we do know that we know him, IF we keep his commandments. **He that saith, I know him, and keepeth not his commandments, is a liar,** and the truth is not in him" (I John 2:3, 4).

Anyone who is professing to follow Christ but is not keeping His commandments is classified by the Bible as a "liar," not a saint.

> "**Keep yourselves** in the love of God, looking for the mercy of our Lord Jesus Christ unto eternal life" (Jude 21).

Why is this passage in the Bible if the entire responsibility for our eternal salvation, after we are once saved, rests upon Christ?

> "We know that whosoever is born of God sinneth not; but he that is begotten of God **keepeth himself,** and that wicked one toucheth him not" (I John 5:18).

From other passages we know that we do not "keep ourselves" in our own strength, but here we are definitely commanded to do our part. It is assuring to note also that when we do our part the wicked one can not touch us.

> "Wherefore the rather, brethren, **give diligence to make your calling and election**

sure: for IF ye do these things, ye shall
never fall: For so an entrance shall be min-
istered unto you abundantly into the everlasting kingdom of our Lord and Saviour
Jesus Christ" (II Peter 1:10, 11).

We cannot go into a study of election but suffice it
to say that when one is elected to a position, or office,
he must accept that position, or office, and fulfill his
duties faithfully, to make his election "sure."

There are three teachings which stand out in this
passage:

1. We do have a responsibility after we are saved.
It is not all left to God.

2. IF we fulfill this responsibility we shall never
fall.

3. Our abundant entrance into the "everlasting
kingdom of our Lord and Saviour Jesus Christ" is con-
ditioned upon our doing our part.

"Let us be glad and rejoice, and give
honour to him: for the marriage of the
Lamb is come, and his wife hath made
herself ready. And to her was granted that
she should be arrayed in fine linen, clean
and white: for the fine linen is the righteousness of saints" (Revelation 19:7, 8).

Our finite minds can not comprehend the over-
whelming wonders God has in store for His own. To
help us understand something of the wonderful exper-
iences in store for us, we, the redeemed ones, are often
referred to as the "bride of Christ." Here we are

spoken of as His "wife." Jesus, through John the revelator, is speaking of the "marriage supper of the Lamb" (verse 9). In preparation for this most wonderful experience we must, with God's help, make ourselves ready. Not all the details of this preparation are given in the passage quoted. From other places in the Bible we learn that the first step is justification. In the passage above, purity of life and righteous living are emphasized. "She (we) should be arrayed in fine linen, clean and white: for the linen is the righteousness of saints."

It is not enough that an earthly bride limit her preparation for her wedding to her outward appearance. It is far more important that her preparation include purity of life and character. The same is true with Christ's bride. Should Christ expect less of His bride than an earthly groom does of his bride?

It is not enough that our righteousness be in Christ. **Christ must be in us.**

What does the Bible say about right and wrong living and their relationship to eternal salvation?

"(For **not the hearers** of the law are just before God, **but the doers** of the law shall be justified)" (Romans 2:13).

"**Not every one that saith** unto me, Lord, Lord, shall enter into the kingdom of heaven; but **he that doeth** the will of my Father which is in heaven" (Matthew 7:21).

"The face of the Lord **is against them that do evil,** to cut off the remembrance of them from the earth" (Psalm 34:16).

"For if ye live after the flesh, ye shall die: but IF ye through the Spirit do mortify the deeds of the body, ye shall live" (Romans 8:13).

"Verily, verily, I say unto you, IF a man keep my saying, he shall never see death" (John 8:51). "And shall come forth; they that have done good, unto the resurrection of life; and they that have done evil, unto the resurrection of damnation" (John 5:29).

"For behold, the day cometh, that shall burn as an oven; and all the proud, yea, and all that do wickedly, shall be stubble: and the day that cometh shall burn them up, saith the Lord of hosts, that it shall leave them neither root nor branch" (Malachi 4:1).

"Who shall ascend into the hill of the Lord? or who shall stand in his holy place? He that hath clean hands, and a pure heart; who hath not lifted up his soul unto vanity, nor sworn deceitfully" (Psalm 24:3, 4).

"Love not the world, neither the things that are in the world. If any man love the world, the love of the Father is not in him. For all that is in the world, the lust of the flesh, and the lust of the eyes, and the pride of life, is not of the Father, but is of the world. And the world passeth away, and the lust thereof: but he that doeth the will of God abideth for ever" (I John 2:15-17).

How can one read the passages above, live in sin, and still think he is on the way to heaven?

"But this thou hast that thou hatest the deeds of the Nicolaitanes, **which I also hate**" (Revelation 2:6).

Who were the Nicolaitanes, whose deeds were hated by both Christ and the church at Ephesus? Weymouth says the Nicolaitanes were "probably an Antinomian sect who divorced ethics from religion and held that conduct did not matter so long as belief was correct."

"But I keep under my body, and bring it into subjection: **lest that by any means, when I have preached to others, I myself should be a castaway**" (R.V. rejected, R. S. V. disqualified) (I Corinthians 9:27).

I recognize there is a difference of opinion as to Paul's meaning. To me it seems clear he is emphasizing the importance of right living as one of the essentials to salvation. Permit me to quote from Adam Clarke's Commentary. "On the subject of the **possibility** of St. Paul **becoming a castaway,** much has been said in contradiction to his own words. He most absolutely states the **possibility** of the case: and who has a right to call this in question?" (Bold-face as in the commentary.)

"**Follow peace with all men, and holiness, without which no man shall see the Lord:** Looking diligently lest any man fail of the grace of God; lest any root of bitterness springing up trouble you, and thereby many be defiled; Lest there be any fornicator, or profane person, as Esau, who

—50—

for one morsel of meat sold his birthright"
(Hebrews 12:14-16).

With the first part of this passage in the Bible,
how can anyone living in sin hope to enter heaven?
Just as Esau sold his birthright, so can a saved man or
woman forfeit eternal salvation for the "morsel of
meat" this world has to offer.

**Is it evident that one must be an "overcomer," or be
faithful unto the end, in order to gain entrance into
heaven?**

"And because iniquity shall abound, the
love of many shall wax cold. But **he that
shall endure unto the end, the same shall be
saved**" (Matthew 24:12, 13).

"And ye shall be hated of all men for my
name's sake: but **he that shall endure unto
the end, the same shall be saved**" (Mark
13:13).

"He that hath an ear, let him hear what the
Spirit saith unto the churches; **He that
overcometh shall not be hurt of the second
death**" (Revelation 2:11).

"**To him that overcometh will I grant to sit
with me in my throne**, even as I also over-
came, and am set down with my Father in
his throne" (Revelation 3:21).

"Blessed is the man that endureth temptation: for when he is tried, he shall receive
the crown of life, which **the Lord hath promised to them that love him**" (James 1:12).

"He that hath an ear, let him hear what the Spirit saith unto the churches; **To him that overcometh will I give to eat of the tree of life,** which is in the midst of the paradise of God" (Revelation 2:7).

"Fear none of those things which thou shalt suffer: behold, the devil shall cast some of you into prison, that ye may be tried; and ye shall have tribulation ten days: **be thou faithful unto death, and I will give thee a crown of life**" (Revelation 2:10).

"But as it is written, Eye hath not seen, nor ear heard, neither have entered into the heart of man, **the things which God hath prepared for them that love him**" (I Corinthians 2:9).

". . . yet now hath he reconciled In the body of his flesh through death, **to present you holy and unblameable and unreproveable in his sight: IF ye continue in the faith grounded and settled, and be not moved away from the hope of the gospel** which ye have heard, . . ." (Colossians 1:21c-23b). (This is an excerpt from one of Paul's long sentences. I suggest you look it up and read the entire seven-verse sentence.)

"And I saw as it were a sea of glass mingled with fire: and **them that had gotten the victory over the beast** and over his image and over his mark, and over the number of his name, **stand on the sea of glass, having the harps of God.** And they sing the song of Moses the servant of God, and the song of the Lamb, saying, Great and marvelous are

thy works, Lord God Almighty; just and
true are thy ways, thou King of saints"
(Revelation 15:2, 3).

The truth in all these passages is summed up by
the words found in one of them, "be thou faithful unto
death, and I will give thee a crown of life" (Revelation
2:10c).

A significant fact is that the admonitions in Revelation are to different New Testament churches.
Therefore they most certainly apply to this dispensation of grace in which we now live.

Are backsliders lost unless they repent?

"Now **the just shall live by faith:** but if any
man draw back, my soul shall have no
pleasure in him. But **we are not of them
who draw back unto perdition:** but of them
that believe to the saving of the soul"
(Hebrews 10:38, 39).

The people referred to here are saved people—"the
just" who are to "live by faith." It is evident that it
would be possible for them to "draw back unto perdition." They are resolved to not draw back unto perdition but to continue to "believe to the saving of the
soul."

Incidentally, **living by faith** shows they are not
expecting Christ to keep them without any effort on
their part.

"**If any man defile the temple of God, him
shall God destroy;** for the temple of God is

holy, which temple ye are" (I Corinthians 3:17).

Paul tells these Christians that they are the temple of God. He also tells them that if they defile the temple of God (themselves) God will destroy them. Every born-again person who goes back to a life of sin is most certainly defiling the temple of God, and thus bringing this condemnation upon himself.

"For this cause, when I could no longer forbear, I sent to know your faith, lest by some means the tempter have tempted you, and our labour be in vain" (I Thessalonians 3:5).

In verse seven of this same chapter Paul addresses these people as "brethren." Again, as when speaking to the Galatians, how could Paul possibly think of there being any chance that his labour might be in vain if none of them could be lost as a result of sin? Paul was concerned lest some of them might go into sin and be lost.

"I am afraid of you, lest I have bestowed upon you labour in vain" (Galatians 4:11).

That Paul is talking to Christian people here is clear from his statement in verse six of the same chapter, where he says "because ye are sons, God hath sent forth the Spirit of his Son into your hearts, crying, Abba, Father." These were people who had been converted as a result of Paul's ministry. If they would still be the possessors of eternal life, in case they went back into sin, why would Paul speak of his labour as having been in vain? As we have seen, Paul expressed the same concern for the Thessalonians.

"And now also the ax is laid unto the root of the trees: therefore every tree which bringeth not forth good fruit is hewn down, and cast into the fire" (Matthew 3:10).

This passage is in harmony with John 15:1-6 where Christ teaches that the unfruitful branches are pruned off and destroyed.

Some of the "trees" referred to in this passage may denote people who have never been saved, and some those who have been saved but have wandered away. Note that they have a common destination. This is also true in the two passages which follow immediately. No distinction is made between the wicked who may once have been saved and those who have never been saved.

"As therefore the tares are gathered and burned in the fire; so shall it be in the end of this world. The Son of man shall send forth his angels, and they shall gather out of his kingdom **all things that offend, and them which do iniquity;** And **shall cast them into a furnace of fire:** there shall be wailing and gnashing of teeth" (Matthew 13:40-42).

"So shall it be at the end of the world: the angels shall come forth and **sever the wicked from among the just,** And shall cast them into the furnace of fire: there shall be wailing and gnashing of teeth" (Matthew 13:49, 50).

"And thou, Solomon my son, know thou the
God of thy father, and serve him with a perfect heart and with a willing mind: for the
Lord searcheth all hearts, and understand-
eth all the imaginations of the thoughts: if
thou seek him, he will be found of thee; but
**if thou forsake him, he will cast thee off for
ever**" (I Chronicles 28:9).

What could be plainer? ". . . if thou forsake him,
he will cast thee off for ever."

"Brethren, **if any of you do err from the
truth,** and one convert him; Let him know,
that he which converteth the sinner from
the error of his way **shall save a soul from
death,** and shall hide a multitude of sins"
(James 5:19, 20).

Notice that James does not consider a backslider
a "sinning saint." To this inspired writer backsliders
are just plain "sinners." Sinners, who MUST be converted if their souls are to be saved from death.

"And if the righteous scarcely be saved,
where shall the ungodly and the sinner
appear?" (I Peter 4:18).

One rendering of the word "scarcely" is "saved
through difficulty." This indicates that the righteous,
in order to be saved, must take their stand for Christ,
withstanding any persecution which may come their
way.

"I am the true vine, and my Father is the
husbandman. Every branch in me that bear-

eth not fruit he taketh away: and every
branch that beareth fruit, he purgeth it,
that it may bring forth more fruit. Now ye
are clean through the word which I have
spoken unto you. Abide in me, and I in you.
As the branch cannot bear fruit of itself,
except it abide in the vine; no more can ye,
except ye abide in me. I am the vine, ye are
the branches: He that abideth in me, and I
in him, the same bringeth forth much fruit:
for without me ye can do nothing. **If a man
abide not in me, he is cast forth as a
branch, and is withered; and men gather
them, and cast them into the fire, and they
are burned**" (John 15:1-6).

From time to time the officials of a church will go
over the membership records and prune the records of
"dead timber," people who no longer qualify as
members of the church. This passage shows that there
is no place for "dead timber" in the true church of
Christ. God the Father, who knows the heart of man,
does the pruning, and He makes no mistakes.

"When **a righteous man turneth away from
his righteousness,** and committeth iniquity,
and dieth in them; **for his iniquity that he
hath done shall he die**" (Ezekiel 18:26).

"When I shall say to the righteous, that he
shall surely live; **if he trust to his own
righteousness, and commit iniquity,** all his
righteousnesses **shall not be remembered;**
but **for his iniquity that he hath committed,
he shall die for it**" (Ezekiel 33:13).

"When the righteous turneth from his righteousness, and committeth iniquity, he shall even die thereby. But if the wicked turn from his wickedness, and do that which is lawful and right, he shall live thereby" (Ezekiel 33:18, 19). "But when the righteous turneth away from his righteousness, and committeth iniquity, and doeth according to all the abominations that the wicked man doeth, shall he live? All his righteousness that he hath done shall not be mentioned: in his trespass that he hath trespassed, and in his sin that he hath sinned, in them shall he die" (Ezekiel 18:24).

"Again, When a righteous man doth turn from his righteousness, and commit iniquity, and I lay a stumblingblock before him, he shall die: because thou hast not given him warning, he shall die in his sin, and his righteousness which he hath done shall not be remembered; but his blood will I require at thine hand. Nevertheless If thou warn the righteous man, that the righteous sin not, and he doth not sin, he shall surely live, because he is warned; also thou hast delivered thy soul" (Ezekiel 3:20, 21).

These passages show that a righteous man may turn from his righteousness, and commit iniquity. They show also that he may die in his sins without repenting. That such a man is lost is evident from the statement that if we do not warn him, his blood is required at our hand.—This book is my warning to all such who will read it.

Yes, the Bible states that the backslider is lost unless he repents.

What are "the wages of sin," and is there any evidence that the unrepentant backslider does not draw these wages?

"Then when lust hath conceived, it bringeth forth sin: and sin, **when it is finished, bringeth forth death**" (James 1:15).

Sin "bringeth forth death," not just loss of reward for the backslider, as eternal security teaches. No evidence here of an exception for anyone.

"What fruit had ye then in those things whereof ye are now ashamed? for the end of those things is death. But now being made free from sin, and become servants to God, ye have your fruit unto holiness, and the end everlasting life. For the **wages of sin is death;** but the gift of God is eternal life through Jesus Christ our Lord" (Romans 6:21-23).

The Roman Catholics developed a system of "dispensations" and "indulgences" whereby, under certain conditions, their members were assured that they would not receive the penalty for sin. The eternal security doctrine approaches this very same practice. It assures its followers that if they once accept Christ they may sin in the future without paying the penalty for sin. Both systems are contrary to the Bible statement, "the wages of sin is death."

What about people who are ashamed of Christ?

> "**Whosoever** therefore **shall be ashamed of me** and of my words in this adulterous and sinful generation; **of him also shall the Son of man be ashamed,** when he cometh in the glory of his Father with the holy angels" (Mark 8:38).

> "For **whosoever shall be ashamed of me** and of my words, **of him shall the Son of man be ashamed,** when he shall come in his own glory, and in his Father's, and of the holy angels" (Luke 9:26).

> "**IF** we suffer, we shall also reign with him: **IF we deny him, he also will deny us**" (II Timothy 2:12).

> "But **he that denieth me before men shall be denied before the angels of God**" (Luke 12:9).

Jesus makes no distinction between the one who has never known Him and the one who has once known Him but later became ashamed to be known as His follower. "Whosoever" includes both.

Is the backslider better or worse off than if he had never been saved?

> "He that despised Moses' law died without mercy under two or three witnesses: **Of how**

much sorer punishment, suppose ye, shall
he be thought worthy, who hath trodden
under foot the Son of God, and hath
counted the blood of the covenant,
wherewith he was sanctified, an unholy
thing, and hath done despite unto the Spirit
of grace?" (Hebrews 10:28, 29).

According to this passage one who was once a
follower of Christ, but who turned traitor to Him, will
be punished to a far greater degree than the one who
has never experienced the way of salvation.

"For if after they have escaped the pollutions of the world through the knowledge of
the Lord and Saviour Jesus Christ, they **are**
again entangled therein, and overcome, the
latter end is worse with them than the
beginning. For it had been better for them
not to have known the way of righteousness, than, after they have known it, to
turn from the holy commandment delivered
unto them" (II Peter 2:20, 21).

Who, except saved people, "escape the pollutions
of the world through the knowledge of the Lord and
Saviour Jesus Christ"? If such people are eternally
saved regardless of the fact that they may be "again
entangled therein, and overcome," why is it said of
them that "it had been better for them not to have
known the way of righteousness"?

What hope is there for the backslider?

"If we confess our sins, he is faithful and
just to forgive us our sins, and to cleanse us
from all unrighteousness" (I John 1:9).

Because of God's love for all of us, including the
backslider, we have this wonderful passage in the
Bible. The backslider comes back to God the way he
came to God in the first place, "confessing his sins."

What do we learn from the parable of the ten virgins?

"And while they went to buy, the bride-
groom came; and **they that were ready went
in** with him to the marriage: and the door
was shut" (Matthew 25:10).

There was a time when ALL of the virgins were
ready. Through neglect, five of them failed to main-
tain this readiness and thus were excluded from the
marriage. "How shall we escape, if we neglect so great
salvation; . . .?" (Hebrews 2:3a).
If the parable of the ten virgins does not teach
that some who at one time were ready for heaven will
fail to enter in, what does it teach? Notice, too, the
words, "and the door was shut," emphasizing their
permanent exclusion.

What do we learn from the prodigal son?

"It was meet that we should make merry,
and be glad: for this thy brother **was dead,**
and is alive again; and **was lost,** and is
found" (Luke 15:32).

Eternal security teaches that all the time he was away from home, the prodigal son was still the son of his father. Physically this is true. Note though that the father considered him as "dead" and as "lost." He was a lost son and it was not until, of his own volition, he repented and returned to his father that he again received any of his father's blessings. His father did not compel him to remain under his protection, nor compel him to return. If he had never returned he would never again have enjoyed his father's home. He would have remained a lost son.

Was Judas Iscariot once a saved man? or what do we learn from Judas Iscariot?

"Jesus answered them, Have not I chosen you twelve, and one of you is a devil?" (John 6:70).

This verse seems to solve the problem of Judas. What more could one expect from a devil? Because of this statement of Christ's, many have concluded that Judas was a devil incarnate. Let's use the same reasoning with Christ's words to Peter, "But he turned, and said unto Peter, Get thee behind me, Satan: thou art an offence unto me: for thou savourest not the things that be of God, but those that be of men" (Matthew 16:23). Would anyone want to suggest that God later used Satan to win three thousand souls for Him on the day of Pentecost? Possibly we should not dispose of Judas with one passage of Scripture only. In Luke 22:3 we read these words, "Then entered Satan into Judas surnamed Iscariot, being of the number of the twelve." We might conclude that from then on he was a devil incarnate, but there are some serious problems with this conclusion. In Matthew 27:3-5 are these words, "Then Judas, which had betrayed him, when he saw that he was condemned, repented himself, and brought again the thirty pieces of silver to the chief priests and elders, Saying, I have sinned in that I have betrayed the innocent blood. And they said, What is that to us? see thou to that. And he cast down the pieces of silver in the temple, and departed, and went and hanged himself." IF Judas had been a devil incarnate he would have gloated over his success in helping to do away with Christ. Can you imagine a devil feeling any sense of remorse because of such a victory?

Another fact about the "devil incarnate" theory for Judas is that Jesus said, ". . . woe to that man by whom the Son of man is betrayed! good were it for that man if he had never been born" (Mark 14:21b). If Judas was a devil incarnate why would Jesus say it would be better for Judas if he had never been born?

No doubt Judas knew of one or more times when the mob was determined to kill Jesus and "He escaped out of their midst," as at Nazareth. It is most likely Judas expected Christ to again use His divine power and escape; thus Judas could make a little extra money and Christ not suffer at the hands of His enemies, either. This is indicated by the words "when he saw that he was condemned." It is evident that Judas did not expect Christ to be condemned.

There is abundant evidence that Judas was an ordinary man, just as were the other apostles. Observe that Judas was one of the twelve apostles. He was more than a disciple. A disciple was a follower of Jesus but an "apostle" was one "sent out with orders." The first part of the tenth chapter of Matthew gives us the names of the twelve apostles. The name of Judas Iscariot "who also betrayed him" is included. Notice, in this same chapter, the "orders" Jesus gave Judas and the other apostles. They were to,

Preach,
Heal the sick,
Cleanse the lepers,
Raise the dead,
Cast out devils (Matthew 10:7b, 8a).

That these apostles, including Judas, were at this time living close to Christ is evident from Christ's statement, "For it is not ye that speak, but the Spirit of your Father which speaketh in you" (Matthew 10:20).

God does not depend upon the devil, or those in the devil's kingdom to do His work. God does not commission devils as apostles. We cannot escape the fact that Judas at this time was a saved man, living close to his Lord, the same as the other apostles. What happened? The Bible is very specific. We read in Acts 1:25 that "Judas by transgression fell."

When Christ gave His twelve apostles the power to do the wonderful miracles listed above He was faithful to them in warning them that even though they were chosen for such a wonderful work, any one of them might fail to continue to follow Him and be lost. He told them, "And ye shall be hated of all men for my name's sake: but he that endureth to the end shall be saved" (Matthew 10:22). There was no salvation promised for any of the twelve who might not "endure to the end." Judas did not endure to the end, and Judas was lost. In the seventeenth chapter of John, verse twelve, Christ refers to Judas as being lost.

How can one explain why Christ would choose, as one of His close followers, one whom He knew would fall into such awful sin? First, let me say most emphatically that man is under no obligation to explain the acts of God. There are many things He has not revealed to us. However, I think I can see one very good reason for Christ selecting Judas as one of His closest followers. Christ knew that Satan would do his best to deceive us by trying to make us believe that if we once were saved we could never be lost. How could Christ teach the fallacy of such a doctrine any more emphatically than by the example of Judas?

Does the word "tasted" in Hebrews 6:4-6 cause this passage to support the eternal security doctrine?

"For it is impossible for those who were
once enlightened, and have **tasted** of the
heavenly gift, and **were made partakers of**
the Holy Ghost, And have **tasted** the good
word of God, and the powers of the world to
come. If they shall fall way, to renew them
again unto repentance; seeing they crucify
to themselves the Son of God afresh, and
put him to an open shame" (Hebrews 6:4-6).

In an attempt to make this passage fit the eternal security doctrine, the word "tasted" is made to mean something less than a real experience. Such an interpretation does not harmonize with "were made partakers of the Holy Ghost." Surely a conflict of meaning does not exist in this Scripture passage.

If the word "taste" must always indicate less

than an actual experience, then in Hebrews 2:9 we learn that Jesus did not really die; He just approached death, or partially died. This passage says, "But we see Jesus, who was made a little lower than the angels for the suffering of death, crowned with glory and honour; that he by the grace of God should taste death for every man."

Eternal security people recognize "taste" or "tasted" as denoting a real experience in such passages as Psalm 34:8, Matthew 16:28, Luke 14:24, Luke 9:27, Mark 9:1, I Peter 2:3, and in the passage from Hebrews quoted in the paragraph above.

In a further attempt to make Hebrews 6:4-6 support the eternal security doctrine the people being described in this passage must be portrayed as unsaved people. They are said to be people who are very much in sympathy with the Christian faith; enlightened people, but not born-again people. I ask, how can we possibly think of unsaved people being made "partakers of the Holy Ghost"? These people even had such a deep experience with God that it is said they had tasted of the "powers of the world to come."

The passage we are studying teaches clearly that saved people may fall away and, by their sins, crucify the Son of God afresh and put Him to an open shame. It also teaches that as long as they continue to do this they must remain outside the kingdom of God.

One illustration from life in one community may throw light upon this last phrase of the passage. I have heard the minister of one of the churches in a certain city tell how in his childhood he was familiar with the Sunday school and teachings of a sound fundamental church. In fact, I understood him to say he attended its services when a boy. I have heard him, from his pulpit, ridicule their faith and teachings and bring down the laughter of his large congregation upon them. In public he denies the virgin birth of Christ, His second coming, a personal devil, and other cardinal principles of the Christian faith. What his early personal experience as a born-again believer may have been, God only knows. He certainly made a profession by faith. This man is "crucifying to himself the Son of God afresh and putting him to an open shame." This passage of Scripture says that as long as he continues to do this it is impossible for him to come back to God.

Does the word "sealed" in Ephesians 1:13 and Ephesians 4:30 cause these passages to support the eternal security doctrine?

"In whom ye also trusted, after that ye heard the word of truth, the gospel of your salvation: in whom also after that ye believed, ye were **sealed** with that Holy Spirit of promise, Which is the earnest of our inheritance until the redemption of the purchased possession, unto the praise of his glory" (Ephesians 1:13, 14).

There are different uses for the word "sealed". It is sometimes used to denote ownership, sometimes to indicate a completed transaction, and sometimes it is used as a mark of approval.

Government officials have seals they place upon documents they approve. Your own church corporation, no doubt, has its seal, which it places upon legal papers to show its approval of transactions. Would anyone suggest that such transactions can never be changed? With every transaction there are conditions to be met. If the conditions have not been met, or are not met, the transaction is not consummated.

To practice such professions as medicine, denistry, law and many others, one must have a suitable document showing that he has qualified according to the laws of his state. On this document is placed the state seal showing that its holder has qualified for such practice. Does this mean a man may continue to practice regardless of his conduct? We all know that the presence of the seal on such a license to practice does not abrogate the state's right to revoke the document because of misconduct on the part of its holder.

God places His seal of approval upon redeemed man, but the Bible is full of conditions and warnings, which if ignored will cause God to withdraw this seal of approval.

"And grieve not the holy Spirit of God,
whereby ye are **sealed unto the day of
redemption**" (Ephesians 4:30).

This passage alone would seem to be enough to convince anyone that the teaching of eternal security is correct. Remember though that in no single passage in Scripture do we find the entire plan of salvation. Were it not for other plain teachings in the Bible, one might conclude this phrase, "sealed unto the day of redemption," indicated an irrevocable act of God. (If you have not yet read the comment on Ephesians 1:13 —just before this passage—it is suggested you do so now. The comment which you will find below is really a continuation of that study.)

I am a teacher, I hold a "Permanent" teacher's certificate. It has the word PERMANENT printed in heavy type at the top. It also bears the seal of the state which issued it. Does this mean that, regardless of how I conduct myself I can still retain my right to teach? Not at all. Every state has its provisions for revoking certificates.

When the seal was placed upon my certificate it was intended that it be for life. So far as the state is concerned it IS for LIFE **provided** I meet certain standards of conduct, throughout my life.

When God places His seal on our lives it is His intention it be "Unto the day of redemption," but He makes it emphatic in numerous places in His Word that He is under no obligation to honor that seal if we break our part of the contract, by living a life which is contrary to His will. In fact, He states clearly He will not permit "anything that defileth, neither whatsoever worketh abomination, or maketh a lie" to enter the City of God (Revelation 21:27b).

What assurance of eternal life may I have?

"Who are **kept by the power of God through faith** unto salvation ready to be revealed in the last time" (I Peter 1:5).

The **unlimited** "keeping power of God" is ours through faith.

"There hath no temptation taken you but such as is common to man: but God is faithful, who will **not suffer you to be tempted**

above that ye are able; but will with the
temptation also make a way to escape, that
ye may be able to bear it" (I Corinthians
10:13).

When God gives us the wonderful promise of not
permitting us to be tempted "above that ye are able to
bear," why should anyone ask for anything more? Do
we have nerve enough to tell God that after He has
made such a wonderful provision for us, we want Him
to save us even though we brush aside His protection
and yield to temptation?

"Now unto him that is able to keep you
from falling, and to present you faultless
before the presence of his glory with
exceeding joy, To the only wise God our
Saviour, be glory and majesty, dominion
and power, both now and ever. Amen"
(Jude 24, 25).
"For the which cause I also suffer these
things: nevertheless I am not ashamed: for
I know whom I have believed, and am per-
suaded that he is able to keep that which I
have committed unto him against that day"
(II Timothy 1:12).

Keep your eye on the ability of God to keep you
from falling. Take advantage of that power of God and
you will live daily with the blessed assurance of eternal life.
(Sometimes the strongest evidence of the fallacy
of a doctrine is found in statements which do not seem
to bear directly upon that doctrine. Such statements
though would have been worded differently if the doc-

trine in question were true. For example, if the eternal security doctrine were correct surely both Paul and Jude would have said "he will keep" rather than "he is able to keep.")

PART III

BASIC DEDUCTIONS
FROM OUR STUDY OF THE
DOCTRINE OF ETERNAL SECURITY

PART III

We can not be ashamed of Christ and deny Him, and still have eternal life.

God provides abundant grace, keeping power and protection, for all who put and **keep** their trust in Him.

The bride of Christ is to be made up of those who **live** for Him; not of those who once lived for Him and later lived for the devil.

When Christ indwells in our lives we experience **full assurance of salvation.** We do not live in fear of being lost. We **know** we are saved.

Many, many passages show that God's salvation is conditional. Only as we meet the conditions, **and continue to meet the conditions,** can we rightfully claim eternal life.

Christ saves us **from** our sins, **not in** our sins. We are righteous and pure before God the Father only when Christ is **indwelling** in us. Christ does **not** indwell in the backslider.

———

Many people confuse **assurance** and **security** (so-called). One may have full assurance of his salvation though he rejects the eternal security doctrine.

———

Numerous passages show the fallacy of the claim that after conversion man has no part in his salvation. We cannot say "Now it is entirely up to God," pay no attention to how we live, and expect to reach heaven.

———

Accept a doctrine only after you have "searched the Scriptures to see if it is so." Don't accept it just because you have heard it preached. You can hear all sorts of conflicting doctrines preached, each of them professing to be Biblical.

———

The Bible teaches that it is possible for one's name to be blotted out of the Book of Life. God is the only one who blots names out. (In a sermon, I once heard a minister say that our names were written in the Book of Life with indelible ink. Does he think that God can't erase indelible ink?)

Christ came and died that we might be made free from sin and live pure lives in the sight of God. Eternal security attempts to provide a way to heaven for the one who is not willing to let Christ come in and cleanse him and keep him clean.

The eternal security doctrine is diametrically contrary to God's attitude toward sin. God abhors sin. Many passages quoted in Part II of this book show that God will not tolerate sin. The Bible is given to us to show us the way to live free from sin, not how to live in bondage to sin.

Christ's sheep will never perish. Christ defines His sheep as those who **follow Him.** While we are His sheep, following Him, we will never perish. If we forsake Christ we are no longer His sheep and do not qualify for the promised protection.

Eternal security emphasizes the supreme sacrifice Christ made on the cross for us, but demands no sacrifice on our part for Christ. It considers a sacrificial life meritorious but not necessary. It ignores Christ's statement, "Whosoever doth not bear his cross, and come after me, **cannot** be my disciple" (Luke 14:27).

In the Garden of Eden Satan told our first great-grandparents, "Ye shall not surely die," if they sinned. Eternal security today is teaching this identical falsehood, "Ye shall not die if ye sin." It was a lie then, how can it be the truth now? God has not reversed His attitude toward sin. **God does not tolerate sin.**

———————

There are many passages in the Bible which pronounce "woe" upon the wicked. Not once do we find even a hint that the backslider is exempt from these woes. On the contrary the Bible teaches that the backslider, unless he repents and comes back to God, will suffer greater "condemnation" than had he never known the saving grace of God.

———————

God loves the backslider. If you are a backslider **God loves you.** He abhors your sins, but He loves you and pleads with you to come back to Him. Come back as did the prodigal son, repenting of the past, forsaking your sins, and pleading God's mercy.

———————

Don't gamble away your soul on a comforting teaching which offers you only a false hope of heaven.

———————

Eternal security attempts to provide a broad way to heaven, so broad that a backslider may take all kinds of sin along with him. It forgets that Christ said, "Enter ye in at the strait gate: for wide is the gate, and broad is the way, that leadeth to destruction, and many there be which go in thereat: Because strait is the gate, and narrow is the way, which leadeth unto life, and few there be that find it" (Matthew 7:13, 14).

It is now time to refer to the four tests for every doctrine as given on pages 28 and 29. Please turn to these tests and read them again.

Does eternal security doctrine pass these four tests?

1. The multitude of Bible passages you have just read show conclusively that the eternal security doctrine does NOT flow from the Bible naturally. These passages show the doctrine is NOT in harmony with the most direct understanding of the entire Bible.

2. It has also been shown that an attempt to support the doctrine of eternal security DOES result in "strained" and "awkward" interpretations of Scripture.

3. We have found that the doctrine of eternal security is NOT in harmony with God's evaluation and abhorrence of sin, and His plan of redemption.

4. It is clear that the doctrine of eternal security does NOT encourage a closer walk with God. On the contrary it teaches that one may wander away from God, engage in the grossest of sins and still consider himself a saved person.

The eternal security doctrine fails to pass a single one of these basic tests.

A CORRECT UNDERSTANDING OF ANY PAR-
TICULAR BIBLE PASSAGE WILL NEVER BE IN
CONFLICT WITH THE CLEAR TEACHINGS OF
THE BIBLE AS A WHOLE.

———————

Is it consistent to teach others a doctrine
which is built upon catchy slogans and a
misunderstanding of certain Bible
passages?

Is it consistent to teach others a doctrine
which minimizes the awfulness of sin?

Is it consistent to teach others a doctrine
which could possibly result in souls being
lost eternally?

ADDENDA

Bible passages to which reference is made
in this book.

In most instances the passages are quoted in full.

King James version, unless otherwise stated.

40 I John 1:6, 7	71 Jude 24, 25
62 I John 1:9	50 Revelation 2:6
40 I John 2:1, 2, 5	52 Revelation 2:7
46 I John 2:3, 4	52, 53 Revelation 2:10;
39 I John 2:5	2:10c
49 I John 2:15-17	31 Revelation 2:11
45 I John 2:24, 25	36 Revelation 3:5
42 I John 3:8-10	51 Revelation 3:21
20 I John 5:11, 12	53 Revelation 15:2, 3
46 I John 5:18	47 Revelation 19:7, 8
41 II John 9	48 Revelation 19:9
35 Jude 5	38 Revelation 21:7
46 Jude 21	70 Revelation 21:27b

These 135 references from 26 different books of the Bible do not include all which might have been used.

Members of Schmul's Wesleyan Book Club buy these outstanding books at 40% off the retail price.

Join Schmul's Wesleyan Book Club by calling toll-free:

800-S$_7$P$_7$B$_2$O$_6$O$_6$K$_5$S$_7$

Put a discount Christian bookstore in your own mailbox.

**Visit us on the Internet at
www.wesleyanbooks.com**

You may also order direct from the publisher by writing:
**Schmul Publishing Company
PO Box 776
Nicholasville, KY 40340**

www.ingramcontent.com/pod-product-compliance
Lightning Source LLC
Chambersburg PA
CBHW071926020426
42331CB00010B/2736